Hospitality Matters
REVIVING AN ANCIENT PRACTICE FOR MODERN MISSION

Courtney Reissig and Scott Corbin, Editors
OWEN STRACHAN, SERIES EDITOR

Danvers Press

Copyright ©2015 by CBMW

All rights reserved. No part of this publication may be reproduced in any form without written permission from the author. Made and designed in the United States of America.

ISBN-13: 978-0692590133
ISBN-10: 0692590137

Scripture quotations are from The Holy Bible, English Standard Version® (ESV®), copyright © 2001 by Crossway, a publishing ministry of Good News Publishers. Used by permission. All rights reserved.

Executive Editor, Greg Gibson
Cover Design by Laura Johns
Layout Design by Mathew B. Sims
www.MathewBryanSims.com

TABLE OF CONTENTS

Theology of Hospitality
SCOTT CORBIN
6

Hospitality Misconceptions
MARY K. MOHLER
11

Children and Hospitality
KRISTIE ANYABWILE
17

Pastoral Hospitality
STEPHEN CRAWFORD
22

Singleness and Hospitality
LINDSAY SWARTZ
28

Me, Hospitable?
COURTNEY REISSIG
35

About the Authors
38

Theology of Hospitality

SCOTT CORBIN

Charging Timothy to shepherd his new flock well, the apostle Paul lists the following requirements that he must discern in newly appointed elders: they must be above reproach, the husband of one wife, able to teach, amongst other things. Yet, what is quite surprising is to find that Paul includes among his various qualifications the requirement that an elder must be *hospitable.*

These qualifications for elders are not the stuff of super-Christians but humble requirements that all Christians ought to pursue. That being the case, we ought to contemplate why that curious qualification—to be hospitable toward outsiders—finds itself among the other commands required of elders.

Christians recognize that God has not only saved us so that we might be saved, but that he has additionally called us to participate in God's reconciling activity through Christ for the world.

For Christians, true participation in this reconciling activity means acts of love displayed toward others that reflect the fullness of the Triune life. In short, it means loving one another through hospitality. As God has been hospitable to us through the giving of his son, so we display God's hospitable love toward others in the giving of ourselves—opening our homes and our hearts toward others.

As we consider what it will mean practically to practice hospitality, we must first consider theologically the dimensions of a hospitable life. In our exploration, we will find that love cultivates generosity which then extends toward others through hospitality.

"WHAT GREATER LOVE THAN THIS?": LOVE

A call to be hospitable is a call to love.

Preceding any hospitable action is a heart that has been sanctified and made alive by the love of God, such that love has overflowed into generosity toward others. Christians fulfill all of the law through love (Rom. 13:10). Christians are called not to love those whom are natural proclivities draw us toward, but also our enemies as well (Luke 6:27-32). Our obedience to the Lord Jesus ultimately finds its wellspring in our love for him (John 14:15). Love is not just an amicable feeling toward others, but the greatest of virtues:

"faith, hope, and love abide, these three; but the greatest of these is love." (1 Cor. 13:13)

Hospitality is love incarnate; the fulfillment of a call to love one another. To be hospitable is to lay one's life down for their friends, an act of sacrificial love on full display. There is an implicit connection between love and service because to serve something is to display our love toward it. "You cannot serve God and Mammon." Why? Because our love to one will display its superior worth in our hearts.

"THAT GOD GAVE US HIS SON": GENEROSITY

The love of God toward sinners in Christ is not just satisfactory, it is abundant—*generous.* So generous that at the heart of the Christian gospel is the bountiful generosity of the Father giving His only Son so that sinners might have life and have it abundantly. It is through the generosity of God that sinners know the fullness of life that there is in Christ.

Likewise, Christians are not just called to give, but to give to others generously. Our hospitality toward the stranger, the alien, and the outcast is such that it looks like waste and folly to the world. Yet, for Christians, the very folly of giving so fully displays the wisdom and kindness of God toward those who were once lost, but are now found.

THE IMPORTANCE OF TABLES: HOSPITALITY

The table metaphor in Christian theology is rich and multivalent. Tables are where enemies become friends. Tables are where dividing walls of hostility are town down. Tables are where generosity is extended toward those who were otherwise excluded. Christians behold God's generosity at the Lord's Table, and extend this generosity toward outsiders with their own tables.

This is why the Lord's Supper, from the beginning, has been so crucial in Christian theology. At the Lord's Supper we see the love of God for sinners, in God's generous giving of His Son for us to feast upon for nourishment. At the Lord's Table, we see the hospitable God extend mercy, though we were by nature children of wrath. We who were once enemies are now friends; we who were once orphans are now children.

Hospitality means homes, and tables, and meals, and joy. It means laughter and tears, sorrow and hope. It means families and friends and shared lives. Through opening our homes, we open our hearts and display the warmth of Christian charity. In our acts of love we push back the darkness with a little more light. In the extra servings of mashed potatoes and blackberry cobbler, the generous, hospitable love of God is made known to a watching world.

For Christians, if we are to continue to retain our prophetic voice to a suffering, decadent culture, we must respond with hospitality—*sanctified* decadence—and a joy that makes even the demons tremble.

INTRODUCING *HOSPITALITY MATTERS*

In the rest of this book, we will be exploring how hospitality shapes who we are as Christians and how we ought to extend this hospitable love toward others. We will look at how this plays out in Christian homes, for women and men, and how we might consider our small acts of hospitable love as larger participation in God's plan to see disciples of Jesus be made and welcomed into the household of faith. We hope that you might begin to consider what it looks like for you, no matter the season, to begin shaping your home and your life toward a hospitable aim.

Hospitality Misconceptions
GETTING TO THE HEART OF HOSPITALITY

MARY K. MOHLER

Hospitality is a massive industry that includes food service and accommodations. Hospitality suites are designated rooms stocked with refreshments and are to be a place that serves speakers and the like by offering many conveniences. One can major in Hospitality Administration at many universities. Yet hospitality of a different nature is a biblical matter as well. It appears four times in the ESV translation of the New Testament as the Greek word, *philoxenia*, which means "love of strangers." Two of the four are simple mandates:

> *"Contribute to the needs of the saints and seek to show hospitality" (Rom. 12:13).*

> *"Show hospitality to one another without grumbling" (1 Pet. 4:9).*

Both Paul and Peter clearly instruct all believers to show hospitality. No qualifications are given for gender, gifting, or availability. Peter included the phrase "without grumbling" as he had certainly heard of complaints among those who have grown weary in providing for the needs of others. We are wise to remember that not only is hospitality often grouped by biblical scholars as a spiritual gift of service, but it is also a command to all believers.

One excellent example of the unique importance of this topic is found in the writings of C.S. Lewis in *The Four Loves*. He inspires us by his analysis of the role of hospitality in the early church:

For we all wish to be judged by our peers, by the men "after our own heart." Only they really know our mind and only they judge it by standards we fully acknowledge. Theirs is the praise we really covet and the blame we really dread. The little pockets of early Christians survived because they cared exclusively for the love of "the brethren" and stopped their ears to the opinion of the Pagan society all round them.

Nothing has changed in terms of our need for affirmation and encouragement from "the brethren." What has changed is our willingness to recognize that fact and act upon it. We are all commanded to joyfully practice hospitality just like the early church did. How grateful we should be that our homes do not resemble the sparse and cramped hovels of biblical times. How sobering it is to realize that the obedience of the early church to this simple command had amazing results.

HOSPITALITY'S MISCONCEPTIONS

It is not uncommon to hear people refer to the seemingly lost art of hospitality. So what changed? The advent of technology brought with it big promises of mass quantities of saved time, but that was a lie. The conveniences are wonderful, but they brought with them less free time and not more. It matters not if we can now prepare a turkey and all the trimmings in just a few hours if we have neither the time, interest, nor skill to do so. Too many women are simply not at home more than a few waking hours per day. They are buried by the demands of working outside the home and running a household such that inviting guests into the chaotic atmosphere is just not going to happen. Others are so overwhelmed by responsibilities across the board that they easily rationalize the fact that they contribute to the greater good in a myriad of ways. They will be only too happy to enumerate those ways, but having guests in their home is just not for them. Still others would be very eager to return to the patterns of their grandparents who welcomed strangers and friends with open arms but sadly, they have absolutely no idea how to do so. Their mothers did not teach them how to cook. They know of no mentors who would be willing to help them now. The thought of embarking on what seems like a daunting task causes them to join the ranks of those who lament that hospitality is clearly a lost art and a faded memory.

One of the best ways for the so-called lost art to be recovered is by modeling hospitality in a host of ways whenever we have the chance. The message needs to be proclaimed loud and clear that there is no singular method used to practice it. Misconceptions abound regarding what it truly entails. Many women who multi-task and brilliantly handle complicated issues seem to fall prey to intimidation when it comes to this topic. Others somehow see it as beneath their level of importance and mentally relegate it to those who like to wear aprons and bake cookies. Is it not paradoxical that the mentality exists where hospitality management is a worthy profession but hospitality at home is for the simple or old fashioned? Satan loves both of these mindsets since the end result means that hospitality is not practiced and opportunities are overtly missed.

HOSPITALITY'S TRUE PURPOSE

Hospitality is not about the provider. It is not about showing how creative, innovative, organized, proficient and gifted one is. Instead, it is about selflessly sacrificing one's time, efforts, and some degree of finances. It is about taking the risk to let your guard down and invite people to get to know you beyond a superficial level. It is about abandoning the sinful tendency to be self-absorbed and instead seek to do whatever is necessary to meet needs.

Another apt definition comes from an unlikely source. I heard about a great-grandmother who was welcoming guests to the town that she had called home for all of her one hundred years on this earth. When someone commented on how welcoming the little berg was, the grandmother quipped, "Well, when you come to our town, we just want you to feel better when you leave than when you came." What a great way to describe biblical hospitality! If you provide a weary traveler with a filling meal, homemade or not, or a warm bed, he will feel better when he left than when he came. If you welcome a friend in crisis into your home and truly listen to her in spite of the fact that your house is not in perfect order, she will feel better when she leaves than when she came. If you pause to help your neighbors and then invite them to your patio to visit and to tell you about themselves, they will feel better when they leave than when they came. Hospitality is not to be equated with five course gourmet meals and formal wear. Hospitality is to be equated with selfless caring for others. Remember that the world is filled with people who feel isolated, lonely and unloved. Simple acts of hospitality can lift one's spirit in amazing ways. We have no idea how the Lord may choose to bless our sincere efforts to produce results beyond what we can ever imagine.

Children and Hospitality

THE DREAM (AND THE REALITY) OF INCLUDING YOUR CHILDREN IN HOSPITALITY

KRISTIE ANYABWILE

We have guests coming over for dinner at 6pm. In my home, we start early Saturday morning, for a day of cleaning. Each of my 3 kids responsible for cleaning their room, a bathroom, and one other common area in the house. My 8 year old son vacuums and takes out the trash, my crafty 15 year old daughter irons the tablecloth, takes out the good china for our French-themed tablescape, my 17 year old daughter helps with dinner. Her homemade French baguette is to die for! My husband spends the day cutting grass, trimming bushes, and watering flowers, taking a few cuttings to place in a vase for our centerpiece. I spend most of the day in the kitchen. Tonight it will be Lyon-inspired summer salad, French onion soup, potatoes au gratin, beef bourguignon, and crème brûlée for dessert. All chores and food are done by 5pm. Everyone hits the shower, and we casually linger around the family room, eagerly awaiting the arrival of our guests. That's the dream.

As we think about including our children in our hospitality, it is easy to have unrealistic expectations about how it is all going to go. So before we get into the practical takeaway for hospitality in the family, here is real life hospitality for my family.

It's a Tuesday morning. As we battle the morning traffic, I ask what we should serve our guests for dinner that night. After suggestions ranging from Chick fil A, to spaghetti (again) to kale salad (from my vegan daughter), I call my hubby (on Bluetooth) who says it's totally up to me as long as I don't experiment on our guests (which I've done plenty of times before and it usually turns out great. Usually). With no help from the peanut gallery, I drop the kids off and hit the grocery store, scanning the hot foods section for ideas. I decide against ham sandwiches and potato salad, and opt instead for a family favorite, a dish we call "yummy chicken" and which you are likely to have on your first dinner at my house. It's easy, pretty quick, and tasty. It can be adapted to any dietary restrictions, except vegan, but we usually have vegan-friendly veggies, a salad and rice or pasta on the side. I grab my ingredients from the aisles, quickly check out, and head home so I can get busy cleaning the house before I cook.

Since I only got to clean upstairs this morning (I had a book lunch date with a friend and battled traffic picking the kids up from school), the morning dishes are piled in the sink, with the dishwasher never unloaded from the night before. So I rush the teens to unload and reload the dishwasher so I can start prepping dinner. I run to clean the downstairs bathroom and yell to my son to grab the vacuum and run over the floors before our guests arrive. I enter the kitchen ready to cook by 5:00, convincing myself I still have plenty of time to prepare dinner, and *all the dishes are still piled high* onto every available counter space, in the sink, and even on the stove. I yell upstairs to the girls asking why the dishes aren't done, and they yell back over Netflix, "We were hungry and needed a snack first". I yell back that our guests will be her in an hour, and I need to start cooking *now*. They saunter downstairs, clear a path for me to get started, and I realize that instead of getting thin cut boneless skinless chicken breast, I had purchased regular boneless chicken, so now I have to pound out eight chicken breasts! If you've ever done this before, you know this is long, hard labor.. I'm pounding the last chicken breast at 5:30pm, when my darling husband walks in from work, sees the chaos, and asks how he can help. I mumble something, which he understands as he should take out the trash, clear the clutter off the dinner table, and quietly play Madden 15 until I yell for something. The chicken is seasoned and breaded, it's now 5:45, and I begin sautéing praying that beastly traffic would hold our guests back by 30 minutes (or an hour). While the first batch of chicken is cooking, I boil water for the pasta and put a can of diced tomatoes and roasted peppers in the food processor for the sauce. I ask my husband to find the kids again so they can set the table and I can run upstairs to pull my hair up and find a fresh shirt—all just in time for our gifts.

We've looked forward to having this couple over, and I try to remember that as I slowly walk down the stairs, catching my breath from the busyness of the day. In the chaos of getting dinner ready, some dinner was lost—but I salvage as much as I can and silently praise God that we seem to have enough ice cream for dessert.

We sit for a lovely time of sharing testimonies, recounting God's grace in our lives, and laughing out loud about momentous nothings. My kids listen politely, speak when spoken to, and slip out to do homework (i.e. Netflix) as soon as they convince the youngest to ask our guests if they can be excused from the table.

Dinner is a success. Fellowship was sweet. New dishes were piled high in the kitchen. I breathe a prayer of gratitude, pick up *Crazy Busy* to see what we'll be discussing next week on my

lunch date, when I realize somehow I had missed reading a chapter in the book, the one entitled "You Need to Stop Freaking Out About Your Kids". So I did. Instead, I recounted all the ways my children were involved in hospitality that day. Instead of expecting a perfect experience, here are some realistic suggestions:
- Ask them for dinner suggestions. Serve something that your guests and your family will enjoy.
- Let them help with chores.
- Enlist them for help in the kitchen. Let them set the table.
- Teach them to serve. Even little ones can get drinks for your guests
- Give them an appropriate time to slip out for homework and to get ready for school the next day.
- Hospitality is an opportunity for them to practice kindness to each other and to your guests, patience in listening, and self-control.
- Your husband is your greatest asset. Use him!

There you have it! Dream on but embrace the reality of a busy life and fold in your children where and when you can. It won't be perfect but it will be worth it.

"Show hospitality to one another without grumbling."

1 Peter 4:9

Pastoral Hospitality
A VISION FOR KINGDOM HOSPITALITY

STEPHEN CRAWFORD

As Christians, we often talk about not letting our Christian worship and devotion be confined to only our Sunday gatherings. As a pastor, it remains one of my jobs to shepherd my people into a vision of taking their Christian life beyond the four walls of a church building and into the streets, workplaces, and homes that mark their Mondays through Saturdays. But the question we often wrestle with is, how? How do we create a sense of continuity between Sunday worship services and the whole of the Christian life? Or, put a different way, how do we battle the sense of discontinuity many Sunday worshippers feel between what happens in sanctuaries on the Lord's Day and the "ordinariness" of the rest of the week? How do we as ordinary Christians allow the sacred to spill over into the everyday?

One answer lies in the way we view our homes and practice hospitality. The act of hospitality allows the sacredness of Christian worship and the reality of the gospel message to bleed over into the everyday, and it causes us to see many of the domestic duties and routine as places where the ethics of the kingdom of God truly take hold of our hearts and lives.

HOSPITALITY SAVES

In a famous passage in Matthew 25, Jesus gives us a picture of what the final judgment will look like. In it, we see Him celebrate and welcome the sheep on his right as those who committed themselves to a fairly basic set of concerns. What is striking about this passage is how radically domestic these concerns are—things like providing food, drink, covering, and company. In fact, four out of the six items Jesus cites would have been traditionally associated almost exclusively with the home.

Cleary Jesus is not saying, "If you do these things, you'll be saved," as though salvation was some works-based system of merit. But what is He saying? He shows us that these simple acts of hospitality condition us into not simply believing in the King, but actually being a kingdom-minded people—people that *get* it, that understand and embody the ethics of this kingdom.

These are the ethics of the kingdom, of course, because these are the ethics of our King. Jesus tells the sheep on His right that this kingdom was "prepared for you from the foundation of the world." We serve an eternally hospitable King. He thought of us *first*. He took care of our well-being *beforehand*. This teaches us something essential to kingdom-minded hospitality.

"PREPPERS"

I've recently become aware of a group of people known as "preppers." These are people who believe that the end of the world as we know it is quickly at hand, and so these people are "prepping" for this doomsday scenario. This means that they are organizing their whole life around the constant looming possibility of a complete and utter societal collapse, and they have prepared themselves with various skills, provisions, weapons, and plans if and when this occurs.

What starts for most as taking a few simple, precautionary steps turns into an all-out obsessive commitment to what is no longer a question of "if" but "when." For "preppers," their engagement in the practices associated with "prepping" causes them to experience an increasingly deeper buy-in to this lifestyle, mindset, and doomsday narrative. With each new piece of survival gear they purchase, with every survival skill they hone, with every "go-bag" they pack, they are literally living out the narrative they have banked their lives on, which of course only serves to buttress their commitment to the certainty of the narrative.

What if we approached having a radical sense of kingdom hospitality like this? Jesus describes for us a coming final judgment, and He is seeking a people who embody this kingdom ethic of hospitality. We therefore need to engage in practices that prepare us for this kingdom so that we're recognizable to our King as He is sorting us out. We need to be "preppers" of a different sort.
As we contemplate the incredible hospitality of our King toward us, and we seek to be a people of kingdom-minded hospitality in the days between Sundays, we need to take on practices and habits that encourage and even require a deeper, more abiding buy-in from us into the lifestyle, mindset, and narrative of the kingdom of God. I'm convinced that the more we take on the practices associated with being hospitable, the more we will embody this kingdom ethic expressed by Jesus in Matthew 25.

THE "HOW"

What practices am I talking about? What habits and lifestyle changes will condition us and point us toward the hospitality ethic of the kingdom? This is where we get practical.

For starters, we could allot more money to our monthly grocery budgets, cook more meals at home to be eaten around our tables, and buy more foods that accommodate more than just our immediate desires and needs. We need to keep our refrigerators and pantries stocked with "social foods," foods conducive to bringing people together so that we're ready at a moment's notice to host people. We need to begin asking the question of ourselves at every supermarket trip, "Who will we be hosting this week?" and shop accordingly. Our practical changes here will cause a deeper buy-in to the mindset of opening your home and welcoming others into your life.

Next, we need to create space around mealtimes in our schedules. We need to stop being satisfied with merely meeting and congregating at neutral "third places" and start seeing our homes and tables and living rooms as sacred places where the kingdom of God is tasted and seen. We need to take on a godly resilience in the face of awkward moments and conversational lulls, and learn the art of having a genuine interest in others.

Additionally, we need to re-think the arrangements of our homes. Where are the screens positioned in your living spaces? How is the seating arranged? What functions as the "center" or focal point of your furnishings? It never ceases to amaze me when I have people over that within the first five or ten minutes they notice (albeit, uncomfortably) that there is no television in sight, and by the end of night, they've expressed a sense of surprised liberation and satisfaction that they were able to fill a whole evening with conversation.

These are just some simple suggestions, and I'm sure many more could be offered. One of the things I hope you'll note, however, is that this is costly. There is no way around it. Kingdom-minded hospitality does not come cheap. But this is the gospel we're talking about here. Our God prepared a place for us with Him in His kingdom, and He secured that place for us by sending His Son Jesus to *die*, remember. The Christian life has always been about God's hospitality at the expense of something costly, God's welcoming of stranger-sinners into His house to dine on the broken body and spilt blood of His Son, and God's consideration of our needs to the neglect of His own. The act of hospitality in so many ways embodies this gospel we profess and believe, and it has the power within it to transform the everyday, ordinary lives we live in our homes into an experience of the kingdom of God.

Singleness and Hospitality
5 HOSPITALITY TIPS FOR SINGLE WOMEN

LINDSAY SWARTZ

Singleness. Ladies, we either love it, hate it, or ride the rollercoaster of both emotions, don't we? One of the questions that tends to jostle our contentment in the midst of this season is: How many areas of life will we miss out on?

The truth is, everyone, regardless of their marital status, is missing out on something. The call of Jesus is a call to miss out in the here-and-now for the sake of future gain. So, there are some things we'll have to wait and pray for. But, there are other areas of involvement, commonly associated with marriage, that don't necessitate it as a precursor. One of these is practicing hospitality.

My ideal hospitality situation would have been in the context of marriage and children. My family would have another family or a group over to our Pinterest-worthy house for a home-cooked meal and an evening of chatting and laughing. The visit would be all the more enjoyable because I had the benefit of tag-teaming it, physically and emotionally, with my husband.

This is why we need to look at hospitality as less of a setting and more as a posture of service we can contextualize. There is no one-size-fits-all when it comes to how to practice hospitality. Since I work full-time outside of my home, I also find I'm short on the time and energy needed during the week to make a nice homemade meal. And more often than not, it's easier for me to go over to my friends' houses because of their kids' schedules than it is for them to come over to mine. This means I'm often not the host, but the guest.

As believers, what we *know* about hospitality is that it's a must. And it sometimes takes a little creativity, mixed with some trial and error, to figure out how to practice hospitality right where we are. Here are several ways I've been able to (imperfectly) engage in hospitality and some that I'm hoping to adopt.

1. HELPING OTHERS CREATE A HOSPITABLE ENVIRONMENT

I've frequently imagined that my home would be *the* go-to place, with people dropping in throughout the week. But, I've spent more time living at *others'* houses, and my address has changed so many times that I have trouble filling out documents that require my last 5 years' worth of zip codes. As a result, my hospitality has been constricted. Not only that, but my personality isn't as naturally extroverted as I once led myself to believe. So, how can I be involved in hospitality in the midst of all this?

I've come to see that one of the ways I can practice hospitality in my vagabond, single years is by helping *others* create a hospitable environment in their home. Whether it's helping a friend cook or clean before a party, taking a turn bringing desserts to small group, or staying later to make sure all the clean up is taken care of, the old adage is true: many hands make light work.

2. REMEMBERING THE LITTLE PEOPLE

Most of my friends' families are pretty close to being complete, while I haven't even had the chance to get started. I'll be honest, that's really hard sometimes. One of the things I've wanted the most is to be able to open my home to children that I can call my "own" — to nurture, care for, and raise them. Yet, there are plenty of ways I can influence children and young ladies, even though none of them are "mine."

For example, I can invest in friends' marriages and children or free them up to counsel another couple by offering to babysit. I can model what a godly woman looks like by spending one-on-one time with my friends' little girls. I can mentor a middle school, high school, or college student that I go to church with. The possibilities are as vast as my willingness to forego my pity parties.

On my worst days, I get stuck in a lament that I don't have children to raise or the reality of the transient nature of many of these relational investments. On my better days, I realize the truth that everything the Lord gives is for a season. So, the question is, what will I do with the unique ability and emotional energy to invest in as many girls' lives as I choose?

3. HOUSING LONGER-TERM GUESTS
Singleness often affords a luxury of freedom that I, alone, get to decide how to use. Whether it's time, possessions, or housing, I don't have to consult anyone else in making my decision. While I have the freedom that many married people miss, I also have an abundance of alone time — more than I care to entertain.

This allows me to open my home — or, apartment — to visitors passing through or to young ladies who need a place to stay for a few weeks or months. Honestly, having strangers in my space isn't always my favorite thing to do. It can be awkward and inconvenient and shows me where I fall short of showing hospitality without grumbling (1 Peter 4:9). But I know the blessing it is — both to me and my guests — through personal experience.

In His Word, God instructs us to actively look for ways to contribute to our brothers' and sisters' needs and to seek to show hospitality (Romans 12:13). This is a way I can proclaim that my time, my home, my possessions, even my plans, are not my own. They belong to the Lord, and I don't want to shrink my soul by being stingy with what He has given me.

4. CREATING A WELCOMING ENVIRONMENT AT WORK

In Christians circles, we often talk about the truth of how marriage sanctifies us because it's a joining of two sinners. And, call me crazy, but I want to experience that.

Instead, God has graciously given me a job in ministry, and I spend most of my day in the office with about 10 co-workers. After a few jobs, I've started to say, tongue-in-cheek, "Who needs marriage when you have co-workers?" Even though I work with believers, the reality is that when you put sinners together for 8+ hours a day, you're going to feel the heat.

Hospitality at work is not unlike hospitality at home. As a Christian who believes that the gospel should affect every area of my life, I can continue to close my heart to those around me, bury my head in the sand, and look out for #1 on my way to success, or I can walk in the Spirit, be kind and tenderhearted (Ephesians 4:32), look for ways to give grace with my words (Ephesians 4:29) and my acts, and show perfect courtesy to my friends (Titus 3:2).

Is my office a safe-haven where my female co-workers can come and find a sympathetic ear, hear truth spoken, and feel encouraged? Do my brothers feel built up by me? Am I a willing, glad-hearted servant? I've failed in these areas, but I pray, by God's grace, I'll leave the fragrance of Christ in the places I work.

5. PRAY FOR OPENNESS AND OPPORTUNITIES

Two of the greatest hindrances to my practice of hospitality are my selfishness and my ignorance. Selfishness is obvious; I see opportunities to show hospitality, but I willingly choose not to engage in them because I'm too lazy, comfortable, or it's not my preference.

Ignorance is more subtle, though. For example, I didn't realize what an opportunity I had for hospitality at work until I started writing this article. I was blinded to it. I also struggle with hospitality in my apartment complex because of my lack of familiarity with certain ethnicities that live around me. I shrink back from extending a hand of friendship for fear of doing something wrong.

Ladies, the Lord sees, knows, and purposes our situation as singles. He's acquainted with the unique joys, challenges, and disappointments we face. He also sees our obedience and faithfulness — however imperfect. Every attitude and act of hospitality, especially toward one of His sons or daughters, is as if it's done to the Son, himself, and pleases our Father greatly (Matthew 25:40). Let's seek His help to use the freedoms and flexibility He's given us in our singleness to create a culture of hospitality wherever we go.

Me, Hospitable?
HOSPITALITY IS FOR EVERYONE

COURTNEY REISSIG

Often when we think about hospitality our mind conjures up images of women hurrying around a kitchen seeking to prepare the perfect Pinterest meal. Women sign up for hospitality classes. Even home economics courses have typically been taught by women with female students filling the classroom seats. The idea of hospitality being a female issue is changing in the larger culture, with men participating in dinner parties and intentional community building around food as much as women have in the past. But in the church, hospitality is a human issue, not a female one.

    I hope you have seen throughout this brief book that hospitality is for everyone—men, women, and children. Scripture reminds us that hospitality is not gender specific. Abraham welcomed the angels who told him of Sodom's coming destruction (Gen. 18:1-15). The widow at Zarephath provided food for Elijah (1 Kings 17:7-

24). Lydia opened her home to the church (Acts 16:13-15). Elders must be hospitable (1 Tim. 3:2). And Jesus, the God-man, came into the world "eating and drinking" as Rachel Jankovic helpfully points out in her book *Fit to Burst*.

The practice of welcoming people into our homes is rooted in our function as image bearers of God. We welcome others—family, strangers, neighbors, enemies—because God stooped low to welcome us while we were still enemies and strangers (Rom. 5:8). We can be hospitable because the God, whose image we bear, was once hospitable to us.

For too long we've relegated the ministry of hospitality to women only. When we minister together, to welcome outsiders into our homes we tell a beautiful story of God's self-sacrificing love for us that we in turn share with others by our very hospitality.

We hope this little book has helped you catch a vision for the ministry of hospitality. It looks different in every home, every season, and every family. It's not a checklist to master, but a lifestyle to adopt. If you walked away from this with a list of things to implement rather than a heart to serve others in your season, we will have not done our job.

Hospitality is not about meeting a list of requirements, but about telling a story of the greatest welcome to every guest who walks through our door. God welcomed us into his family through Christ, so we in turn can do likewise in our own homes, praying that with every hospitable act those we serve will see the light of Christ in our lives and in our families.

About the Authors

COURTNEY REISSIG is a wife, mom, and writer. She is the author of The Accidental Feminist: Restoring Our Delight in God's Good Design (Crossway, 2015). She is also an assistant editor for CBMW. When she is not wrangling three little boys, she enjoys reading, running, and hanging out with friends. She and her family live in Little Rock, AR.

SCOTT CORBIN is currently an M.Div. student at the Southern Baptist Theological Seminary. Before enrolling at Southern, he studied History at Texas State University in San Marcos, TX. He is married to his wonderful wife Jessi and they are expecting their first child in March of 2016.

STEPHEN CRAWFORD serves in ministry at the Austin Stone Community Church and is an MDiv student at Southeastern Baptist Theological Seminary. He and his wife, Taylor, are currently recovering emotionally and financially from

About the Authors

renovating their house in Austin, Texas, where they love to host neighborhood parties and freak out their neighbors by making them cookies, picking up trash in the streets, and extending a general disposition of kind cheerfulness.

KRISTIE ANYABWILE joyfully supports her husband of 24 years, Thabiti, as he pastors Anacostia River Church in Southeast Washington, DC. They have 3 children. Kristie enjoys spending time with family, cooking, and discipling women as well as speaking and writing about marriage, motherhood, and ministry. You can find her at www.iamconvinced.wordpress.com and follow her on Twitter at @kanyabwile.

MARY K. MOHLER serves as the president's wife at Southern Seminary in Louisville, Kentucky and as the founder and director of Seminary Wives Institute. She holds a B.S. in biology from Samford University, and has contributed to several books, including The Christian Homemaker's Handbook (Crossway, 2013). Mary enjoys teaching and mentoring student wives as they prepare for ministry. She and her husband, Dr. R. Albert Mohler, Jr., were pleased to be to receive CBWM's John Piper Award for Complementarian Leadership in 2014. The Mohlers are members of Third Avenue Baptist Church.They are the proud parents of two grown children and a son in law. They will be thrilled to welcome a grandson in the fall of 2015.

LINDSAY SWARTZ currently serves at the Ethics and Religious Liberty Commission (ERLC) as the managing editor of content. She completed her Master of Divinity at The Southern Baptist Theological Seminary. She's navigating single life in her 30's and loves movies, traveling, good food, coffee shops, girly things, and sports. She lives in Nashville, TN and is loving every minute of living in Music City.